ON THE MAP

RUSSIA

Titles in This Series:

Canada   Russia
France   Spain
Italy   U.S.A.
Japan   West Indies

Series editor: Daphne Butler
American editor: Marian L. Edwards
Design: M&M Partnership
Photographs: ZEFA except
Chris Fairclough 16b, 19br, 28bl
Bruce Jamson 15t
Geoffrey Sherlock 16t, 19bl, 21tr, 25br
Spectrum 121, 191, 22br
Map artwork: Raymond Turvey
Cover photo: *St. Basil's Cathedral, Moscow*

Library of Congress Cataloging-in-Publication Data

Flint, David, 1946–
    Russia / written by David Flint.
       p.   cm.—(On the map)
    Includes index.
    Summary: Surveys the geography, natural resources, family life,
food, schools, transportation, leisure time, and famous landmarks
of Russia.
    ISBN 0–8114–2941–5
    1. Russia (Federation)—Juvenile literature.
    [1. Russia (Federation).]   I. Title.   II. Series.
DK510.23.F54   1993
    947–dc20   92–43190
                                           CIP AC

Typeset by Multifacit Graphics, Keyport, NJ
Printed and bound in the United States
  2 3 4 5 6 7 8 9 0 VH 98 97 96 95 94

RUSSIA

David Flint

RSVP
RAINTREE
STECK-VAUGHN
P U B L I S H E R S
The Steck-Vaughn Company
Austin, Texas

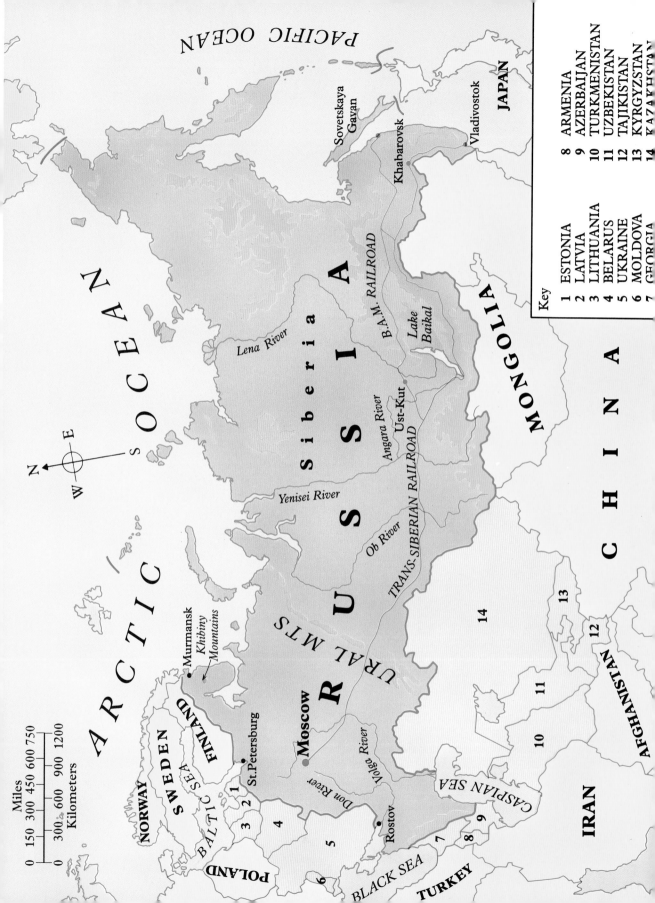

PACIFIC OCEAN

JAPAN

Key

1 ESTONIA
2 LATVIA
3 LITHUANIA
4 BELARUS
5 UKRAINE
6 MOLDOVA
7 GEORGIA

8 ARMENIA
9 AZERBAIJAN
10 TURKMENISTAN
11 UZBEKISTAN
12 TAJIKISTAN
13 KYRGYZSTAN
14 KAZAKHSTAN

Sovetskaya
Gavan

Khabarovsk

Vladivostok

B.A.M. RAILROAD

Lake
Baikal

MONGOLIA

S i b e r i a

Lena River

Angara River

Ust-Kut

TRANS-SIBERIAN RAILROAD

R U S S I A

Yenisei River

Ob River

CHINA

13

14

URAL MTS

11

Murmansk
Khibiny
Mountains

12

ARCTIC   OCEAN

10

N
W   E
S

IRAN

AFGHANISTAN

Moscow

Volga River

CASPIAN SEA

NORWAY

SWEDEN

FINLAND

St.Petersburg

1
2

3

4

5

6

Don River

Rostov

7

8 9

BLACK SEA

TURKEY

POLAND

BALTIC SEA

Miles
0 150 300 450 600 750
0 300 600 900 1200
   Kilometers

Contents

Very Big Country

Russia is a very big country. It covers part of two continents—Europe and Asia. Russia is about twice the size of the United States. It is so large that it covers eleven time zones. When it is 9:00 o'clock in the morning in Moscow in the west, it is 7:00 o'clock at night on Russia's East Coast.

From the West Coast to the East Coast, the country stretches out nearly 6,000 miles. In the east, Russia meets the Pacific Ocean. Much of this region is frozen during winter and cold and foggy in summer. The Baltic Sea is to Russia's west. To the north is the Arctic Ocean. This ocean is frozen for nine months of the year. To the south, Russia joins China and Iran.

Throughout Russia there are cold, snowy winters. Spring comes in a rush in April as ice and snow melt. Summers are short and hot. Much of the country is not used for growing crops. Russia is so far north and has such very cold weather that farming is impossible in many parts. Also the area has a short growing season and little rainfall.

The population of Russia is very large. But the people are not evenly spread out across the country. Most Russians live in the western part of the country.

Murmansk is a busy port in northern Russia.

Snow and ice on Russia's Pacific Coast.

High mountains near Khabarovsk in southeastern Russia.

Wide flat plains cover much of Russia.

The jagged Khibiny Mountains in Russia.

Brown bears find food
near volcanoes.

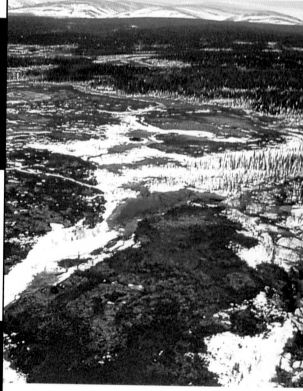

The treeless tundra in
northern Russia.

Tundra, Plains, and Mountains

The tundra covers most of the northern part of Russia. Here the land is mostly flat with occasional hills and low mountains. Bitter cold winters last for at least eight months of the year. Soil is very poor on the tundra. The only plant life is mosses and low shrubs. However, Arctic foxes, reindeer, and polar bears do manage to survive in this environment.

South of the tundra are huge forests of pine, fir, and other trees. This region is sometimes called the Great Northern Forest. Here brown bears, wolves, and lynxes live. Some crops such as wheat and fruit can be grown in the warm months.

To the west are broad, flat plains. It is here that most of the country's farming goes on. Farmers can grow a variety of crops. Crops grown in the west include corn, barley, potatoes, wheat, and sugar beets.

Along Russia's Pacific coast are high mountains and many volcanoes. Very few people live in this part of Russia. Dense forests of oak and maple trees are found here. Railroads link Russia's East Coast to other parts of the country.

Seas, Rivers, and Lakes

Russia has many large bodies of water. The Caspian Sea is part of Russia's southern border. Several rivers, including the huge Volga River, flow into the Caspian Sea. However, no rivers flow out. This is because the Caspian is an inland sea. It is the largest inland sea in the world.

Most rivers in Russia are linked by a series of canals. In eastern Russia, the Ob, Lena, and Yenisei are the largest rivers. They flow north into the Arctic Ocean. In winter, these rivers freeze solid and are used as roads. People can travel across them in sleighs. Floods are common in the spring when the ice begins to melt and run off into the rivers.

Lake Baikal, just north of Mongolia, is Russia's best-known lake. It is the deepest lake in the world. Over 300 rivers flow into it. Even though it is very deep, Lake Baikal still freezes over in the winter. Many varieties of fish, plants, and animals are found in and around the lake. Some of these are not found anywhere else in the world.

Russia's waterways have made travel by boat a very important means of transportation.

Lake Baikal has many fish found nowhere else in the world.

A pleasure boat on the huge Angara River in Siberia.

Bridges across the Don River in the city of Rostov.

Flower sellers help people to brighten their homes all year round.

Red Square outside the walls of the Kremlin is a favorite spot for visitors.

Moscow has both old and brand new buildings.

Moscow

Two out of every three people in Russia live in towns or cities. Moscow, the capital, is the largest and most important city. It began as a small settlement, many, many years ago, in the 12th century. Today, Moscow is the center for government and international trade. The Moscow River, for which the city was named, flows through it.

In the center of Moscow is the Kremlin. The Kremlin is an ancient fortress. It sits on the north bank of the Moscow River. The Kremlin has historic as well as modern buildings. There are palaces, churches with onion-shaped domes, and government buildings.

Outside the Kremlin walls is a large plaza called Red Square. Parades are sometimes held in Red Square.

Moscow has been called the city of museums. Its galleries contain paintings, priceless jewels, and other works of art. The city is also famous for the Bolshoi Ballet and the opera.

Throughout Moscow are many gardens and parks. The most famous is Gorki Park. People flock to Gorki Park year round. They enjoy activities such as boating, skating, tennis, and soccer.

Natural Resources

Russia is a country full of natural resources. A great deal of all the world's forests are in Russia. That makes lumbering one of the country's major industries. Trees are cut down to make furniture, paper, and toys. Russia has vast resources of coal, too.

Siberia, in eastern Russia, is a storehouse of riches. It has large supplies of oil and natural gas. Great deposits of iron, gold, silver, and diamonds are also found in Siberia.

Most Russian people live in the western part of the country. The natural resources are found in the east. In between are thousands of miles of frozen land. Railroads have been built to link east and west. Rivers connect the north and south. Together, rivers and canals form a major transportation network. Also, the rivers are a great source of electric power.

For many years very few people lived in Siberia. The harsh weather and bad roads made living conditions nearly impossible. In recent years Siberia has seen many changes. For example, new factories have been built. People have moved there to mine the resources and to work in the factories. Entire towns of new, modern homes have grown up in Siberia.

Russia's forests are a source of valuable wood.
In winter local people go cross-country skiing through the forests.

Underground heat, beneath volcanoes,
can be used to make electricity.

Russia's scientists are also trying to
use the tides to generate electricity.

Most Muscovites (people from Moscow) live in small apartments in tall apartment buildings.

A family meal—tea is poured from a small decorative urn, which is called a samovar.

Family Life

Most people in Russian towns and cities live in rented apartments. These are usually just two small rooms. Many homes are shared by two families. Some newly married couples have to live with their parents for several years. This is because there is a shortage of new apartments and houses. People who live in the countryside have small wooden houses or log cabins.

Many households often include grandparents. They sometimes serve as babysitters for working parents. In most families both parents work. Because housing space is limited, grandparents sometimes must share a room with the children.

Although their homes are small, most families have a television set, refrigerator, and a washing machine. One family in six has saved enough money to buy a car. The majority of people depend on public transportation to get from place to place.

Children are at the center of family life. Parents work hard to give their children as many things as they can. They are encouraged at an early age to get involved in music, dance, or sports. Each year hundreds of young children try to get into the best dance and music schools.

Shopping and Food

The Russian people spend a lot of time shopping because there are long lines in most stores. On an average, they spend fourteen hours a week shopping for food and other needs.

Sometimes shoppers can buy a wide range of foods from meat to fruit and cheese, or bread and fresh vegetables. But often, there is a shortage of food, so people have to wait in long lines.

The average family eats a lot of bread and potatoes. A typical breakfast consists of bread, butter, and jam. Adults drink tea and children drink milk. Lunch is mostly soup and bread.

Meat or fish is eaten for dinner. Fish is very popular in Russia. Fishing in the nearby seas and distant oceans adds to the food supply. In addition to potatoes, the people eat vegetables, such as beets, cabbage, and tomatoes.

Shoppers often wait in long lines for other goods, too. Clothing, shoes, and many household items are in short supply. Russia is working hard to increase the production of food and housing to meet the needs of the people.

Waiting on line to buy things in stores is part of everyday life for Russian people.

The huge GUM deparment store in Moscow is always crowded.

Sausages are a popular food and are made in many different types.

Going to School

Education is very important in Russia. All children must go to school for eleven years. They start at age seven and go until they are seventeen or eighteen.

In most families both parents work full-time. Nursery schools care for young children until they are three. After that children go to kindergarten until they are seven and ready for first grade.

Children go to school six days a week. The school day starts at 8:30 A.M. and lasts until 1:30 P.M. in the afternoon. There is one short break in the morning. In the afternoon older children play sports or study in their classrooms. Some children go to special schools to study music, ballet, or languages.

After ninth grade students can continue secondary school or go to technical or trade schools. These schools train them to work as technicians and workers in farming, engineering, and industry. Some schools offer evening courses for working students.

Students who have done well in elementary and secondary school can take a test to enter a university. In Russia, schooling is free from first grade through the university.

Russian children wait to greet a visitor with flags and flowers.

Some large farms have their own schools like this one.

School children visit memorials like this one in Moscow. The flame burns to remember people who died in the World War II.

The traditional reindeer-pulled troika sleigh is ideal for getting around in the snow.

Nuclear-powered icebreakers keep a sea-lane open in the short Arctic summer.

Ten lanes of traffic on one of Moscow's busy streets.

Getting Around

Russia is a vast region of mountains, plains, and rivers. Getting around in such a country has always been a problem. The mountains, earthquakes, floods, and cold winters make travel difficult.

Rivers have always been Russia's lifelines. Long ago Russian cities began on river trade routes. Today, these same rivers are important to transportation. Large rivers like the Volga carry coal and steel. Special built icebreakers keep the ports and rivers open, especially in the north. Rivers are the main highways going from north to south.

Railroads are the main east to west connection. They link cities across the country. The Trans-Siberian and the Baikal-Amur Mainline (BAM) railroads link Moscow with the eastern part of the country.

Travel by air is becoming more important to Russia. Airplanes connect all major cities. Small airplanes fly to places that cannot be reached by road.

Away from towns and cities, people still use sleighs called **troikas** to get around in winter. Horses or reindeer are used to pull the sleighs. Many families enjoy this as a form of recreation.

Work

Out of every five workers in Russia, one is a farmer, two work in factories, and two work in shops and offices. Most Russian women work. They do many of the same jobs that men do.

Only ten percent of Russia's land is used for farming. In many areas it is too cold or too dry to grow many crops. The best farmland is in the southwest. Although cold, the winters there are not as harsh as in other parts of the country. The warmer summers make it possible to grow some grains and vegetables.

While some field work is done by machines, much is still done by hand. Large farms are being divided up and sold to small groups of farmers.

Russia has many factories. Electric power from rivers and lakes supplies factories with energy. Everything from textiles and steel to machinery and chemicals is made in factories. Recently, more radios, televisions, and cars have been made to meet people's needs.

Russia is a leading oil-producing country. Once the harsh weather made it difficult to get to the large oil reserves. Today, pipelines bring oil to people and factories in all parts of the country.

Engineering and machine building industries are very important in Russia.

Russian farmers still need many more modern machines like these.

Women often do heavy jobs like working on the docks.

Leisure Time

Russians spend their leisure time in a variety of ways. Sports play a big role in the life of most Russian people. Children begin playing sports in nursery school. Over 70 million people belong to exercise clubs. There are also hundreds of free swimming pools and places to work out. Russia's long winters make skating and skiing possible from November to April.

Most towns have sports centers and stadiums where events are held throughout the year. The most popular team sport is soccer. Almost every Russian city has a soccer team. Volleyball and basketball games also draw thousands of fans.

On weekends people like to visit the countryside or entertain friends and relatives. Watching television is a very popular way to spend an evening at home. Movies are popular, too. Every year Russia makes over 120 motion pictures. Huge crowds attend every ballet and opera. There are always lines of people waiting to get into museums and art galleries.

Chess is a national passion. It is played by people of all ages. People can be seen playing chess in parks and on street corners. Crowds stand around carefully watching every move.

Large sports stadiums like this one in Moscow help young athletes.

The Bolshoi Ballet in Moscow is a world famous ballet company.

Many people go to summer camps like this one in Karelia.

Famous Landmarks

The Kremlin is at the heart of Moscow. A fortress has existed on the site since the 12th century. Inside its walls are government buildings and several old cathedrals. Also, a museum is in the palace of the former Russian kings who were called czars.

Many Russians spend their vacations on the Black Sea.

Gorki Park lies along the bank of the Moscow River in the center of Moscow

A Russian Orthodox church service in St. Petersburg.

The splendid St. Basil's Cathedral is next door to the Kremlin in central Moscow.

The beautiful Winter Palace in St. Petersburg has become the Hermitage. It provides a home for the art collection started by Catherine the Great in the 18th century.

Facts and Figures

Russia-the Land and People

Population:	147,400,000
Area:	6,591,104 square miles
Length north-south	6,000 miles
Width east-west	3,200 miles
Capital City:	Moscow
Population:	8,800,000
Language:	Russian
Religion:	Russian Orthodox but other religions practiced
Money:	Ruble which is divided into 100 kopecks

Russia-the Country

1696-1725	Peter I creates Russia as a country with St. Petersburg as the capital
1918	Bolsheviks create the Russian Soviet Federated Socialist Republic with Moscow as the capital
1922	Union of Soviet Socialist Republics (USSR) formed
1991	Russia becomes an independent nation.

Russian Alphabet

АБВГДЕЖЗИЙКЛМНОПРСТУФХ

ЦЧШЩЪЬЫЬЭЮЯ

абвгдежзийклмнопрстуфх

цчшщъьыьэюя

Further Reading

Books

Davis, James E. and Sharryl Davis Hawke. *Moscow.* "World Cities" series. Raintree Steck-Vaughn, 1990

Feinstein, Stephen C. *Soviet Union in Pictures,* "Visual Geography" series. Lerner, 1989

Murphy, Claire Rudolph. *Friendships Across Arctic Waters.* Lodestar, 1991

Audio-Visuals

National Geographic Children's Films.
    Russia, "Families of the World" series. 15 min. Color, 1987

Index

©1992 Simon & Schuster Young Books